DRAWING WITH Sports Illustrated KIDS

by Anthony Wacholtz

illustrated by Erwin Haya and Mike Ray

CAPSTONE PRESS
a capstone imprint

TABLE OF CONTENTS

FOOTBALL

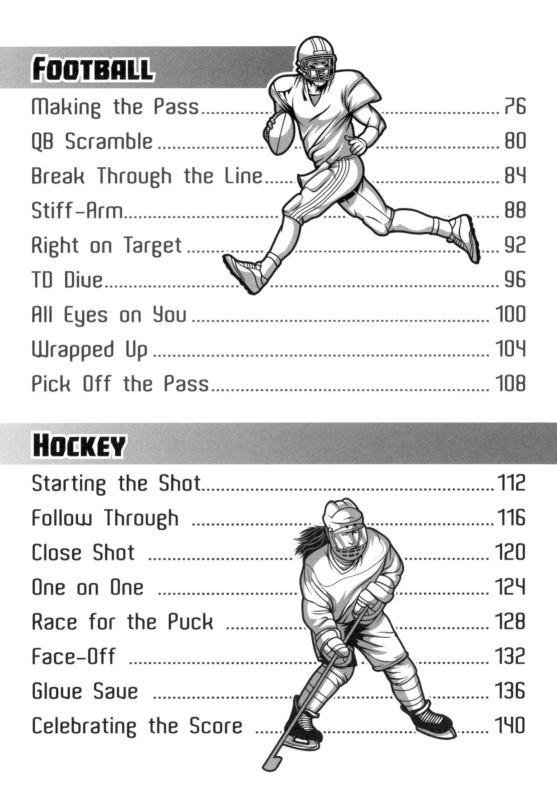

HOCKEY

DRAW YOURSELF INTO THE ACTION!

Have you ever imagined hitting a grand slam, stopping a lightning-fast slap shot, or draining a game-winning jump shot? You don't have to imagine it anymore—all you need is a pencil! With just a few steps, you can put yourself onto the field, rink, or court with your favorite players.

You hit a line drive to the right field corner. Are you fast enough to beat the throw to third base?

You race down the court with only one defender between you and the hoop.

You dunk the ball with a one-handed slam.

You look for an open receiver as a defensive lineman is about to pounce.

CRUNCH!

One of your linemen throws a block that gives you time to fire off a pass.

You fight for control of the puck in front of the opposing team's goalie. With a flick of your wrists, you send the puck past the goalie and into the back of the net.

GOAL!

SUPPLIES AND TIPS

BEFORE YOU STEP INTO THE ACTION, GRAB SOME SUPPLIES:

1. First you'll need drawing paper. Any type of blank, unlined paper will do.

2. Pencils are the easiest to use for your drawing projects. Make sure you have plenty of them.

3. It's easier to make clean lines with sharpened pencils. Keep a pencil sharpener close by.

4. As you practice drawing, you'll need a good eraser. Pencil erasers wear out very quickly. Get a rubber or kneaded eraser.

5. When your drawing is finished, you can trace over it with a black ink pen or a thin felt-tip marker. The dark lines will make your drawing jump off the page.

6. If you decide to color your drawings, colored pencils and markers usually work best. You can also use colored pencils to shade your drawings and make them more lifelike.

Once you've finished a sketch, don't forget the final touches. Do you want the player to look like you or a friend? What team name and number do you want on the jersey? Get creative and make your drawings unique!

Use your imagination and go beyond the illustrations in the book. Give your basketball player a wild hairdo that flies outward as he goes up for a dunk. Sketch flames on the blade of your hockey player as she swings her stick for a shot. You could even combine sports by having a charging running back crash into the catcher during a close play at the plate.

THE SKY'S THE LIMIT!

MAKING CONTACT

You were waiting for it: a belt-high fastball down the middle. You bring the bat around and feel the ball squarely hit the barrel. This ball's going for a ride!

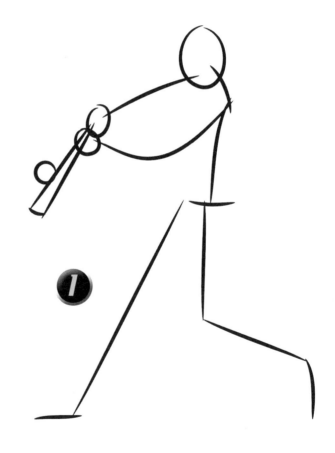

HOME RUN

Crack! You watch the ball soar after a mighty swing. Nothing left to do but start your home run trot!

1

STAY IN FRONT

Crouched down, legs apart, two hands on the ball. There's no way this grounder's getting past you!

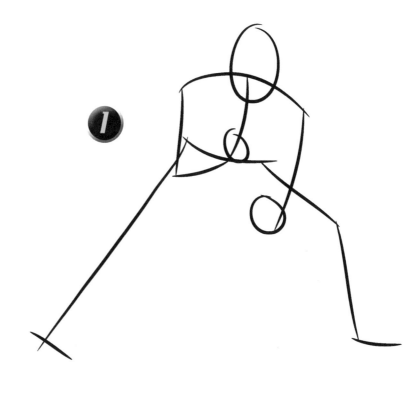

1

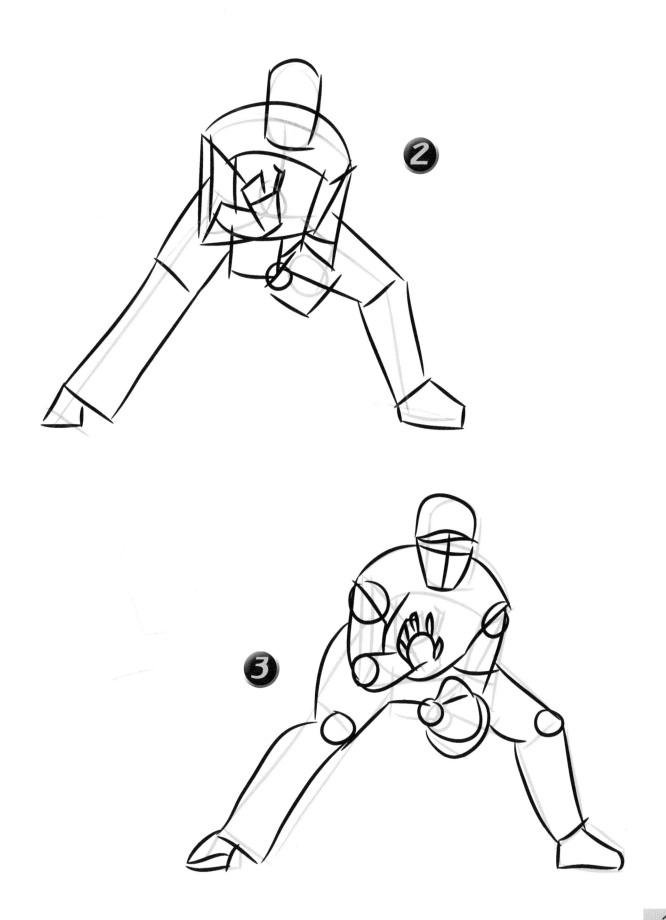

❺

MAKE THE THROW

You've fielded the ball, but that's only half the play. You plant your feet and cock your arm back to throw. You'll have to fire the ball to first to beat the runner and get the out!

⑤

Down THE LINE

The ball jumps off the bat and screams down the left field line. With lightning-fast reflexes, you leap toward the ball with your arm extended. What a play!

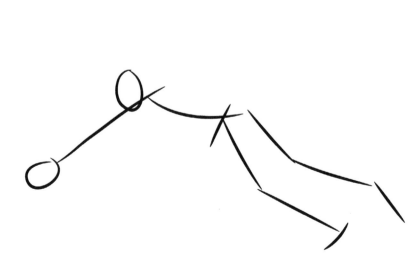

①

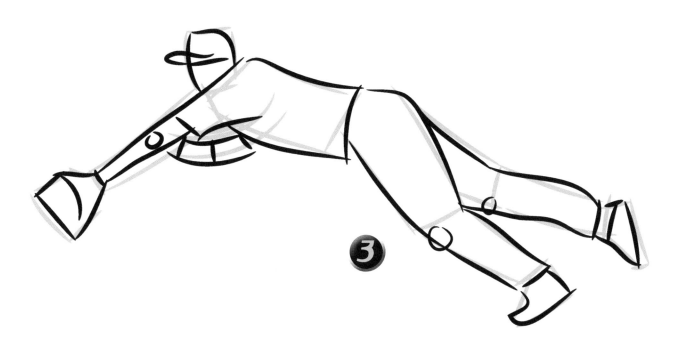

5

PLAY AT THE PLATE

Here comes the relay! The throw is right on target. It's up to you to make the catch and tag out the runner!

DOUBLE THE OUTS

The shortstop lobs the ball to you as you step on second. Spinning in midair, you fire off a quick throw to the first baseman. Double play!

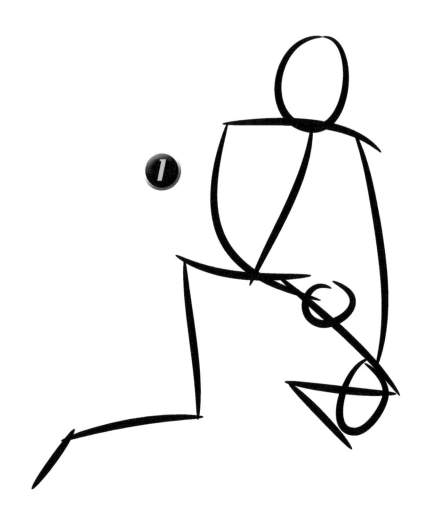

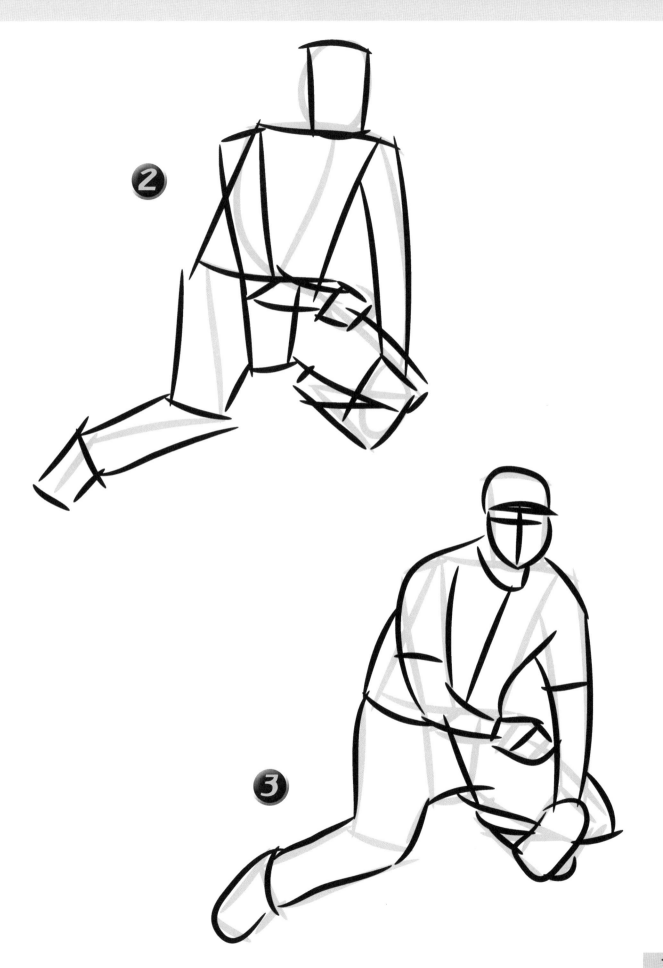

ROBBING HOMERS

A deep fly ball sends the other team into a cheering frenzy. But it's not gone yet! You scale the wall and reach back with your glove. You can't wait to see the instant replay!

1

THE WINDUP

The catcher gives you the sign. After checking the runners, you go through your windup and release the pitch. The moment it leaves your fingers, you know it's a strike.

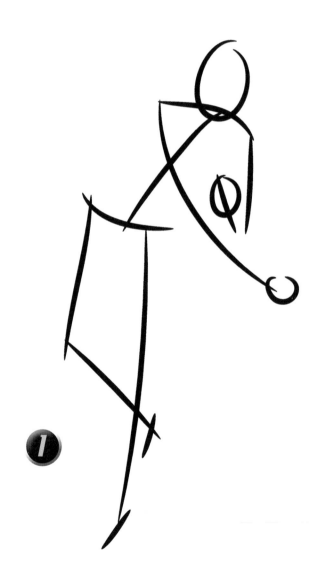

1

PULL-UP JUMPER

The point guard passes the ball to you on the perimeter. The ball leaves your hands, soaring over the defender's outstretched arm. Swish!

1

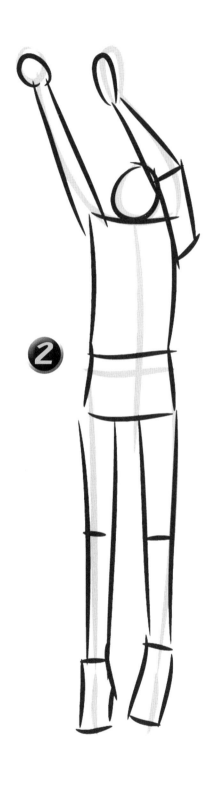

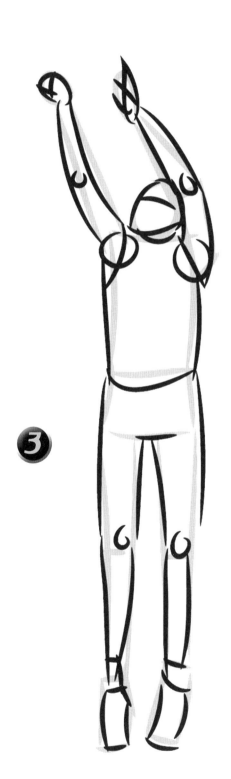

LAY IT UP

Fast break! There's nothing but open space between you and the hoop. You float gracefully toward the basket and lay it in for an easy two.

1

SLAM DUNK

Ready for takeoff! As you hit the peak of your jump, you bring your arms above your head. With both hands on the ball, you're set to jam the ball through the hoop.

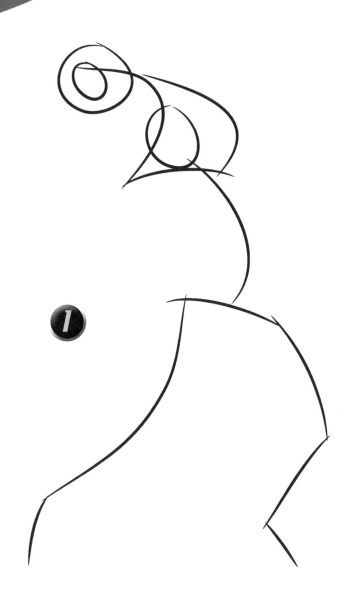

①

ALLEY-OOP

You make a break for the basket, and the point guard sees you take off. He hoists a pass toward the hoop, and you snag it in midair. You bring your arms around for a slam dunk, finishing off a perfect alley-oop.

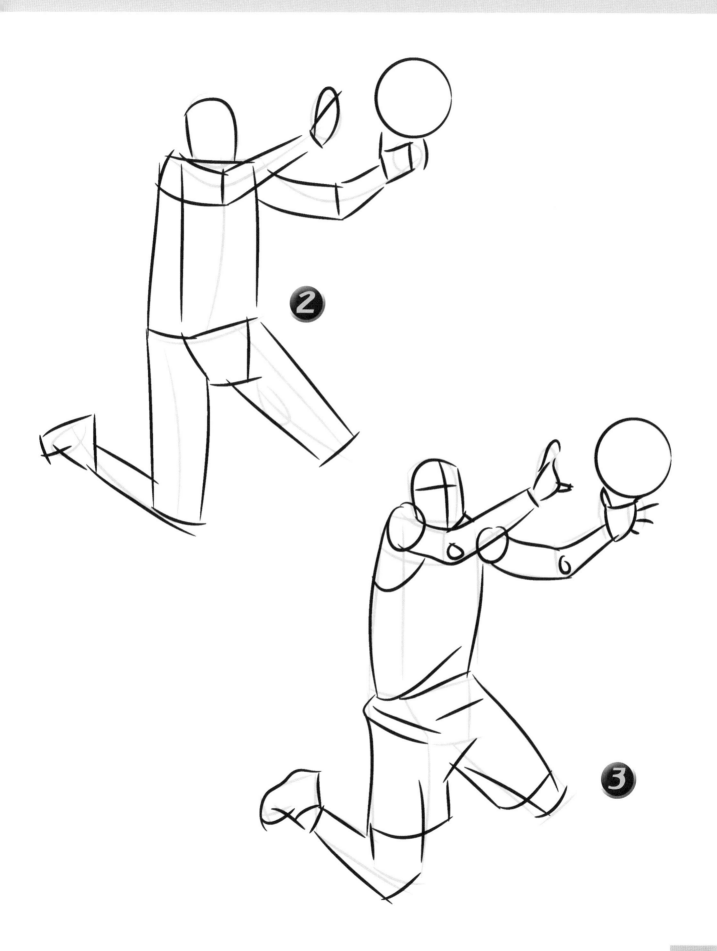

MIDAIR SAVE

The ball bounces off a teammate's hand and toward the sideline. Not so fast! You jump toward the crowd while grabbing the ball. In the blink of an eye, you turn and fire a pass to a teammate. What a save!

4

NO-LOOK PASS

You bring the ball up the court as your teammates start the play. You keep your eyes forward as a teammate breaks to the left. You send him a no-look pass—the other team never saw it coming!

①

2

3

SHOT BLOCKER

A player from the other team goes up for a shot, but you are ready for him. You jump and extend your arm, reaching for the basketball. Your entire palm covers the ball for a successful block. Rejected!

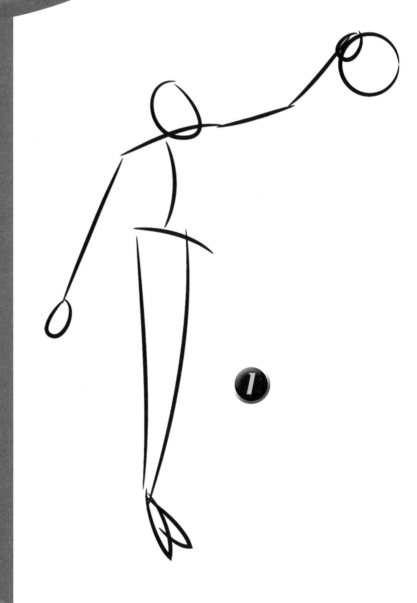

1

DOUBLE-TEAMED

You've lit up the scoreboard all game, and the other players have their eyes on you. As soon as you receive a pass, another defender runs over. You secure the ball with both hands and look to pass.

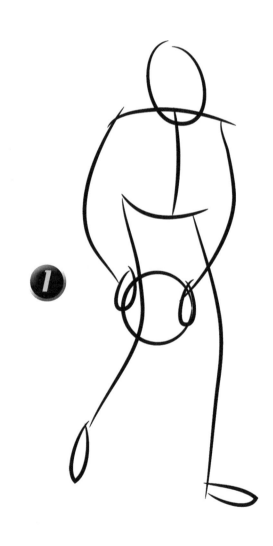

1

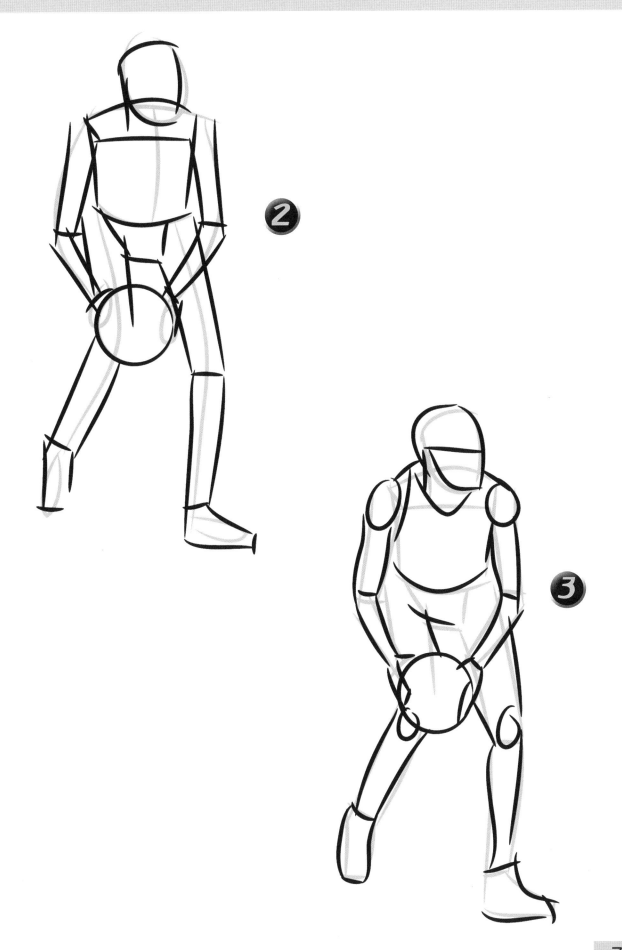

MAKING THE PASS

You drop back to pass and see an open receiver downfield. You'll have to fire off the pass before you get sacked!

1

⑤

QB SCRAMBLE

The pocket has collapsed! You'll have to scramble. Let's hope you can buy enough time for a receiver to get open!

BREAK THROUGH THE LINE

You find a hole in the line and start to race through. You make a cut as defenders miss their tackles. What a move!

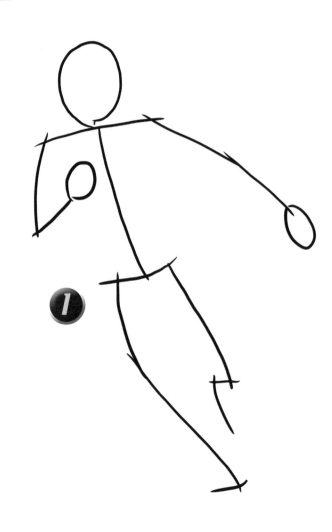

1

4

STIFF-ARM

There's only one defender left to beat, but he's right on top of you. Get ready to stiff-arm him!

RIGHT ON TARGET

You run your route and beat your defender. You turn your head just as the pass drops in front of you. Perfect timing!

1

TD DIVE

You're so close! The end zone is yards away. You dive forward with your arms stretched out, trying to carry the ball over the goal line. Touchdown!

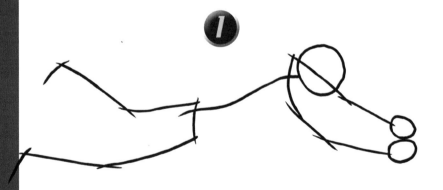

1

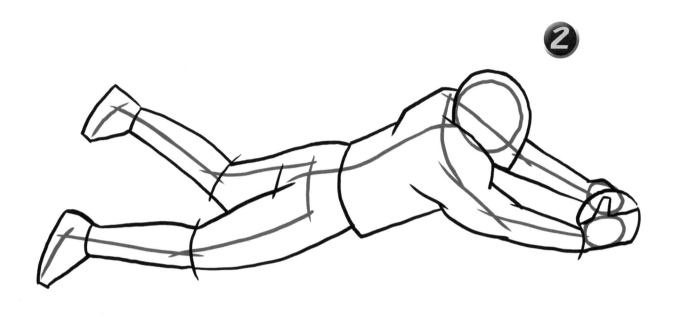

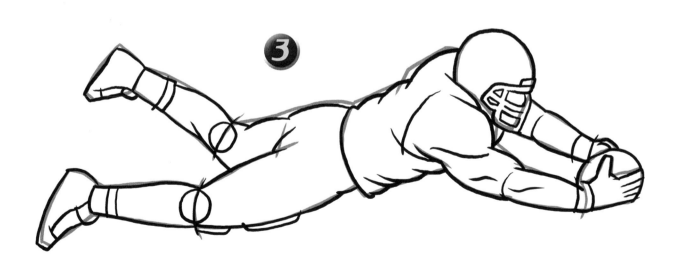

⑤

ALL EYES on You

You've scored a touchdown, and it's your moment in the spotlight. How will you celebrate?

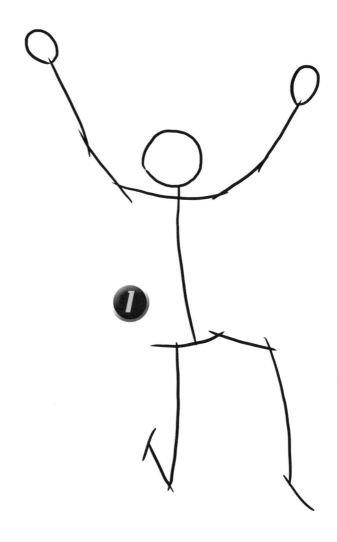

WRAPPED UP

The running back isn't going anywhere! Just as he hits his stride, you send him flying backward with a powerful tackle. They won't run that play again!

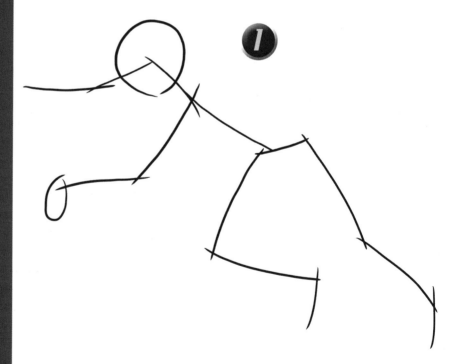

1

PICK OFF THE PASS

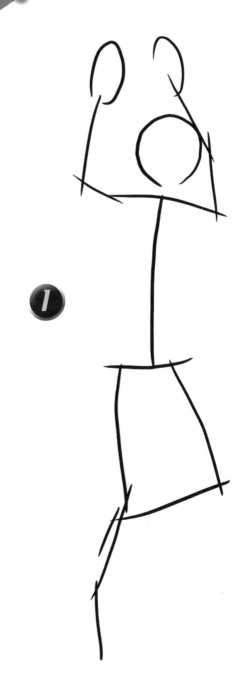

You've read the quarterback's eyes perfectly— the ball's going to your receiver. With a few quick steps, you launch into the air. You've got the position, the higher jump, and now the ball. Interception!

1

2

3

STARTING THE SHOT

You bring your stick back as you keep your eyes on the puck and square up toward the goal. Excellent form for a powerful shot!

FOLLOW THROUGH

You extend your arms forward through the shot, and the puck blasts toward the goal. The goalie will need a good glove—and some luck—to stop it!

1

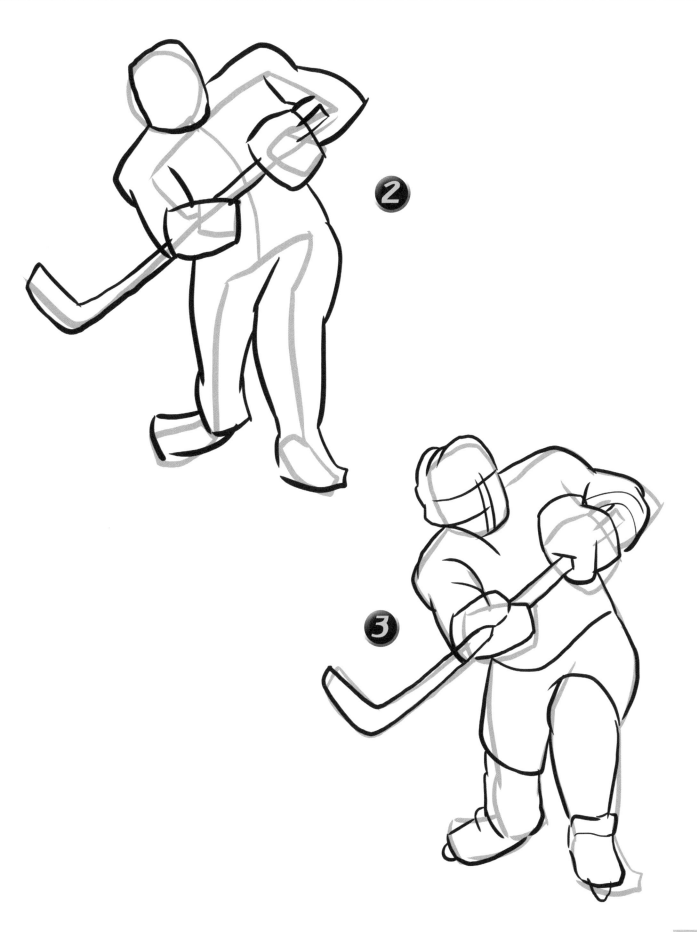

4

CLOSE SHOT

You squeezed past the defenders and received the puck near the goal. Do you have what it takes to sneak a shot past the goalie?

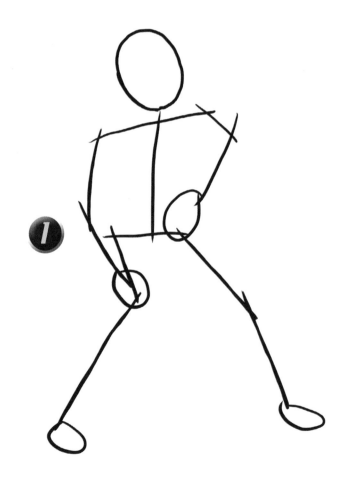

1

One On One

You speed across the open ice with the puck. The only player left to beat is the goalie. You deke to the left, leaving the goalie flailing on the ice. Goal!

2

3

RACE FOR THE PUCK

The puck slides by everyone and ends up at the edge of the rink. You start skating furiously toward the puck, but two opposing players are right beside you. Who's going to get to it first?

1

⑤

FACE OFF

You're hunched over, stick down, eyes focused on the ice. You'll be ready to move as soon as the referee drops the puck. Game on!

1

GLOVE SAVE

The puck hurtles toward the net after a powerful slap shot. With lightning-fast reflexes, you reach out with your glove and snag the puck out of the air. What a save!

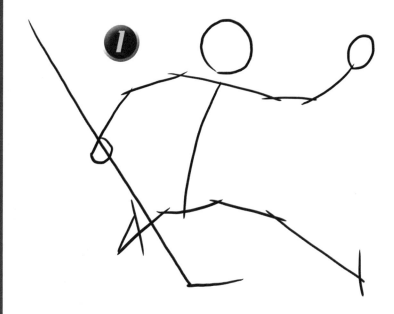

1

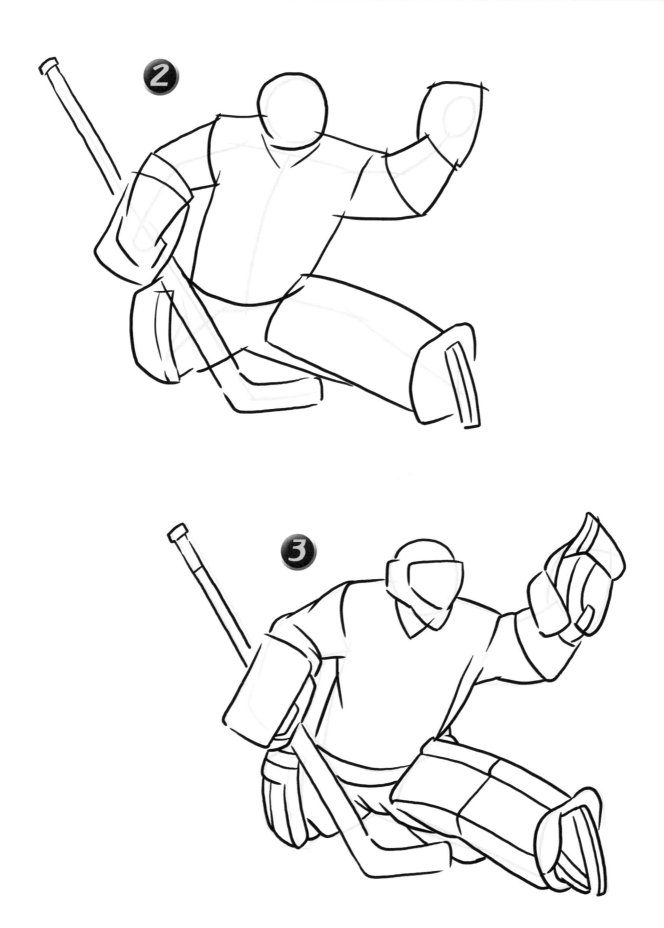

CELEBRATING THE SCORE

It's overtime—the next goal wins the game. Your teammate dishes a pass to you by the net, and you slide it behind the goalie and into the net. Victory!

1

Drawing with Sports Illustrated Kids is published by Capstone Press, 1710 Roe Crest Drive, North Mankato, Minnesota 56003
www.capstoneyoungreaders.com

Library of Congress Cataloging-in-Publication Data
Wacholtz, Anthony.
Drawing with sports illustrated kids / by Anthony Wacholtz.
pages cm
ISBN 978-1-4765-3581-4 (paperback)
1. Sports—Juvenile literature. 2. Drawing—Juvenile literature. I. Title.
GV705.4.W33 2014
796—dc23   2013017524

Editorial Credits
Tracy Davies McCabe, designer; Eric Gohl, media researcher; Eric Manske, production specialist

Photo Credits
Sports Illustrated: Al Tielemans, cover background (bottom right), 15, 19, 23, 47, 67, 71, 83, 91, 103, 111, Bill Frakes, 75, Bob Rosato, cover background (bottom left), 4 (right), 27, 55, 95, 107, Damian Strohmeyer, cover background (top right), 35, 59, 123, 127, David E. Klutho, cover background (top left), 4 (left), 5 (right), 43, 119, 131, 135, John Biever, 39, 87, John W. McDonough, 31, 51, 63, Robert Beck, 5 (left), 11, 115, 139, 143, Simon Bruty, 79, 99

Printed in the United States of America in Stevens Point, Wisconsin.
032013   007227WZF13

144